PREFACE

In today's digital age, IGNOU BCA Computer Basics and PC Software Previous Year Unsolved Papers BCS 011 a solid understanding of computer basics and proficiency in PC software is not just an asset but a necessity. The world is increasingly becoming more connected, and computers are at the heart of this technological revolution. The course BCS-011, "Computer Basics and PC Software," offered by IGNOU, is designed to equip students with the foundational knowledge required to navigate and excel in this digital landscape. This book, **"IGNOU BCS-011 Computer Basics and PC Software Previous Years Unsolved Papers"**, serves as a comprehensive resource aimed at helping students prepare effectively for their exams by providing a collection of carefully selected unsolved papers from previous years.

The objective of this book is to offer students an opportunity to test their knowledge and understanding of the subject matter. By working through these unsolved papers, students can assess their grasp of key concepts, identify areas where they need further study, and develop the problem-solving skills necessary for success in their exams. The unsolved papers included in this book cover a broad range of topics, from the fundamentals of computing to more specific software applications, providing a well-rounded preparation for the course.

Moreover, the format of the questions in this book closely mirrors the structure of the actual examinations, providing students with a realistic experience of what to expect on exam day. This familiarity with the exam format helps reduce anxiety and boosts confidence, enabling students to perform better. The book also encourages a self-directed approach to learning, allowing students to explore different methods of problem-solving and to think critically about the questions posed.The value of this book extends beyond mere exam preparation. It serves as a tool for continuous learning, allowing students to revisit key concepts and refine their understanding even after they have completed the course. For educators, this book offers a rich repository of exam-style questions that can be used to create practice tests, assignments, or as a basis for classroom discussions.

BACHELOR OF COMPUTER APPLICATIONS (Revised)

Chapter 1: Term-End Examination, June, 2014, BCS-011

BCS-011: COMPUTER BASICS AND PC SOFTWARE

Time : 3 hours

Maximum Marks : 100

Weightage : 75%

Note: (i) Question No. 1 is compulsory.

(ii) Attempt any three Questions from the rest.

1. (a) What is LAN ? Explain with the help of diagrams, any two LAN topologies. Also mention their advantages and disadvantages. 7

(b) Explain Von-Neumann architecture with the help of suitable diagram. 5

(c) Explain distributed and Real-time operating system. 6

(d) Explain Sequential Access and Random Access methods for accessing informationfrom memory devices. 6

(e) Differentiate between the following : 6

(i) System software vs. Application software.

(ii) Compiler vs Interpreter.

(f) Explain the following terms : 10

(i) Modem

(ii) Repeaters

(iii) Bridge

(iv) Network Interface Card

(v) Assembler

2. (a) Explain any two Guided and any two Unguided Transmission channels, with the help of diagrams. 10

(b) Explain the purpose of open source software. Discuss any one model ofdevelopment of open source software. 5

(c) What is DNS ? Explain its use with the help of an example. 5

3. (a) Describe Editors and Debuggers as programming softwares. 4

(b) What is Perverse Software ? Explain any four malware. 6

(c) Explain with the help of examples the following conversions : 10

(i) Decimal to Binary

(ii) Binary to Decimal

(iii) Hexadecimal to Binary

(iv) Binary to Hexadecimal

4. (a) What is Internet ? Describe the TCP/IP Model. 7

(b) Explain Data Compression and Disk Management utility in windows. 6

(c) What is Project Management ? Discuss how scheduling and calculation of critical path activities are performed using this software. 7

5. (a) What are flow charts ? What are the basic flow chart symbols ? Draw a flow chart that calculates the area of a circle. 10

(b) What is Hard Disk Drive ? Describe the Storage Organization of a HDD with thehelp of a diagram. 6

(c) Differentiate between a CRT and a LCD monitor. 4

BACHELOR OF COMPUTER APPLICATIONS (Revised)

Chapter 2: Term-End Examination, December, 2014

BCS-011 : COMPUTER BASICS AND PC SOFTWARE

Time : 3 hours

Maximum Marks : 100

Weightage : 75%

Note: (i) Question No. 1 is compulsory.

(ii) Attempt any three Questions from the rest.

1. (a) What is a computer system ? Explain Von-Neumann architecture of computer systems with the help of a diagram. 7

(b) What is a flow chart ? Draw a flow chart to find the average of three given natural numbers. 7

(c) What is open source software ? Explain open source development model. 7

(d) What is software project management ? Explain the following with respect to software project management :

(i) Scheduling

(ii) Timesheet Management

(e) What is Internet ? Explain the basic structure of Internet with the help of a diagram. 7

(f) What is social networking ? Briefly explain its advantages and disadvantages. 6

2. (a) What is URL ? Explain the parts of a URL with the help of an example. 7

(b) What is ASCII ? Explain how Unicode is different from ASCII. 6

(c) What is a motherboard ? List and briefly explain any five parts of a motherboard. 7

3. (a) What is the need of memory hierarchy in computer systems ? Compare magnetic memory with semiconductor memory in terms of speed and cost. 6

(b) What are malwares ? Explain any three malwares, in brief, with the help of an example of each. 7

(c) What is a Compiler ? How is it different from Interpreter ? List any two high level languages, that use a Compiler. 7

4. (a) What is a Web Browser ? Explain how a Web Browser works. Also, explain the types of Web Browsers. 8

(b) What is a programming language ? Briefly explain the following elements of a programming language : 6

(i) Variable

(ii) Data type

(c) What is an operating system ? Explain the following functions of an operating system : 6

(i) File Management

(ii) Memory Management

5. Explain any five of the following with the help of an example/diagram, if needed : 5x4=20

(i) Input Output Devices

(ii) Binary Number System

(iii) Utility Software

(iv) Spreadsheet

(v) Object Oriented Language

(vi) Networking Devices

(vii) Search Engine

BACHELOR OF COMPUTER APPLICATIONS (Revised)

Chapter 3: Term-End Examination, June, 2015

BCS-011 : COMPUTER BASICS AND PC SOFTWARE

Time : 3 hours

Maximum Marks : 100

Weightage : 75%

Note: (i) Question No. 1 is compulsory.

(ii) Attempt any three Questions from the rest.

1. (a) Convert the following hexadecimal numbers to equivalent binary and decimal : 4

(i) (F4) 16

(ii) (AC)16

(b) A 3 inch diameter disk per track has8 plates (16 recording surfaces), 256 sectors per track, 4096 tracks per surface, 512 bytes per sector. Calculate thedisk capacity in GB. 6

(c) What is a flow chart ? Draw a flow chart to find the maximum of three given natural numbers. 6

(d) What is a laser printer ? Compare its features with an ink-jet printer.

(e) What is a desktop computer ? Give a generic configuration of a desktop computer. 5

(f) What is E-mail ? Explain how an E-mail account is created. Also list the folders available in an E-mail account. 7

(g) What is E-learning ? What are its advantages and disadvantages ? List the steps of the process of creating of E-learning content. 6

2. (a) What is data communication ? Explain data communication process with the help of a diagram. 7

(b) What is a device driver ? Are device drivers hardware dependent ? Justify your answer. List four devices which require device drivers. 6

(c) What is a subroutine ? Explain the steps of subroutine execution. Write a subroutine to find the sum of two given positive integers. 7

3. (a) Explain OSI reference model of computer network. 7

(b) What is a search engine ? Explain three categories of search engines. 8

(c) Explain any five major areas of application of computer systems. 5

4. (a) What is main memory ? Differentiate among RAM, Semiconductor memories and Cache memory. 5

(b) What is application software ? How is application software different from system software ? List the names of two application and two system softwares. 10

(c) What is wild ? Explain the characteristics of wild. Explain the uses of wild for a university. 5

5. Explain any five of the following with the help of an/a example/diagram, if needed : 5x4=20

(i) Collaborations with the context of Internet

(ii) LAN and WAN

(iii) Basic Storage Devices

(iv) Disk Management

(v) Computer Virus

(vi) Software Licensing

(vii) Object Oriented Language

BACHELOR OF COMPUTER APPLICATIONS (Revised)

Chapter 3: Term-End Examination

December, 2015

BCS-011

BCS-011 : COMPUTER BASICS AND PC SOFTWARE

Time : 3 hours **Maximum Marks : 100**

Weightage : 75%

Note: (i) Question No. 1 is compulsory.

(ii) Attempt any three Questions from the rest.

1. (a) Draw a flow chart to input a natural number, such as 997, and determine whether or not it is a multiple of 3. 6

(b) In a local area network of star topology, one component failed, bringing down the ' whole network. Predict which component has failed. Justify your answer. 5

(c) Describe two similarities and two differences between a router and a gateway. 4

(d) What is a Wild ? How does it promote content creation by the community ? 5

(e) Explain the Von Neumann's architecturewith the help of a diagram. 5

(f) Describe if statement. Write an if statement to multiply even numbers by 3 and odd numbers by 4. 5

(g) What is a trackball ? How does it work and where is it used ? 5

(h) What is an operating system ? What are its functions and uses ? Name any one proprietary and one open source operating system. 5

2. (a) Describe the layers of TCP/IP reference model. 8

(b) What is a defragmentation utility and what does it do ? What are the benefits of defragmentation ? 6

(c) What are the threats to security from the Internet ? What are the mechanisms available to safeguard oneself from them ? 6

3. (a) What is the use of a compiler in a computer system ? How is it different from an interpreter ? 4

(b) What are the components of the process for developing e-learning content on any subject ? Describe briefly the activities carried out in each, with the help of a diagram / example. 10

(c) Why is a memory hierarchy used in a computer system ? Explain the memory hierarchy diagrammatically, giving the changing characteristics of the memory as we traverse the hierarchy. 6

4. (a) What is meant by mailmerge ? Describe the concept by giving the steps involved in sending a letter to the students of a class giving their grades in different subjects. 8

(b) Describe the features, mechanisms, advantages and limitations of each of the following data transmission media : 12

(i) Twisted Pair Cable

(ii) Microwaves

(iii) Infrared

5. Explain any five of the following with the help of diagrams and examples as appropriate : 5x4=20

(a) Unicode

(b) Arrays

(c) Simplex, Half Duplex and Full Duplex Communication

(d) Firewall

(e) Laser Printer

(f) Table of Contents in Microsoft Word

BACHELOR OF COMPUTER APPLICATIONS

(BCA) (Revised)

Chapter 4: Term-End Examination, June, 2016

BCS-011 : COMPUTER BASICS AND PC SOFTWARE

Time : 3 hours

Maximum Marks :100

(Weightage : 75%)

Note: (i) Question No. 1 is compulsory.

(ii) Attempt any three Questions from the rest.

1. (a) What are the features available in fifth generation computers ? 5

(b) What is a subroutine ? How is it different from a function ? 6

(c) Draw a flow chart to input two numbers and print their arithmetic mean. 6

(d) Describe the different kinds of computer monitors. 6

(e) What is a DNS ? How can an address like. 5

(f) Convert the following decimal numbers to hexadecimal numbers as well as binary numbers 6

(i) (3203) 10

(ii) (4312)10

(g) A company has an office at Delhi and another at Mumbai. It has a good link that delivers 2 Mbps between them. It is required to transfer 8.5 GB of data urgently from Delhi to a computer at Mumbai. A courier can reach the airport and board a flight in 2 hours. The flight time to Mumbai is another 2 hours and he can reach the Mumbai office from the airport in another 2 hours. Which method would be faster — use the link or send a courier ? 6

2. (a) What is open-source software ? What is open-source software licensing ? Describe the open-source development model. 8

(b) List with reasons any six precautions you would take while browsing a website. 6

(c) Describe the constituents and functions of the Central Processing Unit of a computer. 6

3. (a) What is a search engine ? Describe how different actions allow you to conduct a search on any given topic. 10

(b) What are the limitations of a computer ? 4

(c) Describe three key distinguishing features of Object Oriented Languages. 6

4. (a) Explain, with the help of a diagram, the 7-layer OSI networking model. Indicate the function of each layer with an example. 8

(b) Describe the functions and features of the following : 12

(i) Linker

(ii) Debugger

(iii) Device Driver

5. Explain any five of the following with the help of diagrams and examples as appropriate : 5x4=20

(a) Uniform Resource Locator

(b) ROM

(c) Memory Management in an Operating System

(d) Client-Server Architecture

(e) Analogue and Digital Signals

(f) Disk Checkers

BACHELOR OF COMPUTER APPLICATIONS

(BCA) (Revised)

Chapter 5: Term-End Examination, December, 2016

BCS-011 : COMPUTER BASICS AND PC SOFTWARE

Time : 3 hours

Maximum Marks :100

(Weightage : 75%)

Note: (i) Question No. 1 is compulsory.

(ii) Attempt any three Questions from the rest.

1 (a) Convert the following hexadecimal numbers to equivalent decimal numbers and binary numbers :

4

(i) (79)16

(ii) (AC) 16

(b) What will be the storage capacity of a 2.5 inch diameter disc pack having 4 plates, 150 sectors per track , 2048 tracks per surface with each sector capable of storing 1024 bytes?

6

(c) Discuss the uses of various components of a computer as defined in Von Neumann architecture.

4

(d) Explain Compilers, Debuggers, Linkers and Text Editors in the context of programming software.

6

(e) What is an algorithm ? What is the relation between a flow chart and an algorithm ? Draw a flow chart to find the sum and average of marks of a student in 5 different subjects. Marks are given out of 100.

8

(f) Which of the following is a valid Internet Protocol Address ? Justify.

3

(i) 192.168.5.512

(ii) 172.-2.1.0

(iii) 56.26.257

(g) What are the advantages of using Local Area Networks ? List the characteristics of LANs. How are Wide Area Networks different from Local Area Networks ?

7

(h) What is a web browser ? Why is it needed ? Name at least three popular web browsers.

3

2. (a) What is memory hierarchy ? Explain with the help of a diagram. Why is memory hierarchy created in a computer system ?

7

(b) What is perverse software ? List various types of perverse software. Give four ways to counter perverse software.

8

(c) Explain any five features of a spreadsheet software.

5

3. (a) An organization designs and develops programs as projects. The progress of projects needs to be monitored in terms of content and finance. Recommend some application software for the organization. Also explain the features of this software related to various phases of the software development.

10

(b) What is wiki ? List the characteristics of wild. Can wild be used for collaboration ? Explain.

5

(c) What is MOODLE ? Discuss the merits and demerits of E-Learning.

5

4. (a) What are different types of optical disks ? Explain their features and give their advantages. .

8

(b) Explain at least four important features of the following software applications :

12

(i) E-mail

(ii) Database

(iii) Word Processing

5. Explain any five of the following with help of an example/diagram, if required : 4 x 5 = 20

(a) The activities/actions performed by a search engine

(b) Use of subroutines and functions

(c) TCP/IP model

(d) Security threats on Internet

(e) Batch systems and Time sharing operating systems

(f) Diagnostic tools in a computer

(g) Mainframe computers and Supercomputers

BACHELOR OF COMPUTER APPLICATIONS
(BCA) (Revised)

Chapter 6: Term-End Examination, June, 2017

BCS-011 : COMPUTER BASICS AND PC SOFTWARE

Time : 3 hours

Maximum Marks :100

(Weightage : 75%)

Note: (i) Question No. 1 is compulsory.

(ii) Attempt any three Questions from the rest.

1. (a) Convert the following decimal numbers to binary number and hexadecimal number :

6

(i) 57

(ii) 0.215

(b) How is the access time on a disk defined ? Explain the components of access time with the help of an example.

5

(c) Explain the components of a memory system and, the role of cache memory in the memory hierarchy.

5

(d) List any four application softwares. Explain the purpose of each.

6

(e) Draw a flow chart for a program that calculates the area of a circle.

6

(f) What is a Blog ? What are the merits and demerits of blogging ?

4

(g) List three categories of a search engine with the help of an example. What is indexing in the context of a search engine ?

5

(h) Explain the advantages and disadvantages of e-learning.

4

2. (a) What is an Operating System ? List and explain any four services/functions of an operating system.

6

(b) What are the characteristics and advantages of a Local Area Network ? Explain any one LAN topology with the help of a diagram.

8

(c) Define the term 'Open Source Software'. Explain any two important features of the model used for open source software development.

6

3. (a) Discuss the following in brief :

8

(i) Assembler

(ii) Editor

(iii) Interpreter

(iv) Compiler

(b) What is port ? Explain the characteristics of Parallel, Serial, USB and Small Computer System Interface ports.

8

(c) What are the security threats related to Internet ? How can they be prevented ?

4

4. (a) What is data transmission channel ? Compare and contrast Guided and Unguided channels.

4

(b) Compare and contrast the following :

12

(i) SRAM versus DRAM

(ii) SIMM versus DIMM

(iii) ROM versus PROM

(iv) CD-ROM versus USB Drive

(c) What is a URL ? Explain with the help of a an example, the need of DNS in Internet.

4

5. Explain any five of the following with the help of an example/diagram, if required :

5x4=20

(a) Network Interface Card

(b) Word Processing

(c) Collaboration in the context of Internet

(d) Router and Switches

(e) Activities in Software Project Management

(f) Two Data Entry Devices

(g) Cookies in the context of Browser Software

BACHELOR OF COMPUTER APPLICATIONS

(BCA) (Revised)

Chapter 7: Term-End Examination, December, 2017

BCS-011 : COMPUTER BASICS AND PC SOFTWARE

Time : 3 hours

Maximum Marks :100

(Weightage : 75%)

Note: (i) Question No. 1 is compulsory.

(iii) Attempt any three Questions from the rest.

1. (a) Convert the following decimal numbers to binary number and hexadecimal number : 4

(i) 125

(ii) 0.025

(b) Define the term Main Memory. List the differences between RAM and ROM. 4

(c) Define the terms Tracks, Sectors and Cylinders in the context of a hard disk. A disk pack has 12 platters (plates) having 2048 tracks on every surface. It can store 1024 bytes per sector (assume each track has 512 sectors). Calculate the storage capacity of this disk in gigabytes. 6

(d) List two functions of File management and three functions of Memory management systems in the context of Operating systems. 5

(e) What is the role of a Compiler in a. computer ? How is a Compiler different from an Interpreter ? 5

(f) List the advantages of using formulae and macros in a spreadsheet software. 3

(g) For the following IPv4 subnet masks, what would be the size of Net ID and Device ID ? 4

(i) 255.255.0.0

(ii) 255.255.255.0

(h) What is LAN ? What are the advantages of LAN ? 5

(i) What are the features of a browser software ? 4

2. (a) What is a Parallel port ? How is it different from a Serial port ? For connecting a printer, which of the two (serial/parallel) ports will be preferred ? Justify your answer. 6

(b) Draw a flowchart to find the sum of the first n natural numbers. 8

(c) What is a Wiki ? What are its characteristics ? How can it be used for educational purposes ? Explain with the help of an example. 6

3. (a) What is meant by Open Source Software ? Explain the developmental model and licensing of open source software. 6

(b) Explain the uses and functions of the following networking devices : 8

Modem

Repeater

Router

Gateway

(c) What are the various components of a CPU ? Explain the role of each component. How is a CPU interfaced with memory ? Explain. 6

4. (a) Differentiate between the following : 6

(i) Packet and Circuit switching

(ii) Full-duplex and Half-duplex data transmission

(iii) Twisted pair and Optical fibre cable

(b) Explain the advantages of source data-entry devices. Describe the features of any three source data-entry devices. 8

(c) Explain the features of Procedural Programming Languages with the help of an example. How is Object Oriented Programming different from Procedural Programming ? 6

5. Explain any five of the following with the help of an example/diagram, if required : 5x4=20

(a) Disk Defragmenter

(b) Workstation

(c) CD-ROM Disk Layout

(d) Advantages of e-mail

(e) Two-Tier Client-Server Architecture

(f) Features of Project Management Software

(g) Moodle

(h) DNS

BACHELOR OF COMPUTER APPLICATIONS

(BCA) (Revised)

Chapter 8: Term-End Examination, June, 2018

BCS-011 : COMPUTER BASICS AND PC SOFTWARE

Time : 3 hours

Maximum Marks :100

(Weightage : 75%)

Note: (i) Question No. 1 is compulsory.

(ii) Attempt any three Questions from the rest.

1. (a) Convert the following binary numbers to equivalent decimal and hexadecimal numbers : 4

(i) (1011 0101) 2

(ii) (0010 1110)2

(b) Explain static RAM and dynamic RAM. How are they different from each other ? 5

(c) Explain the concept of von Neumann architecture with the help of a diagram.

(d) Draw the flow chart to find if a given number is divisible by 2 or not. 6

(e) Explain the role of a linker and text editor software. 4

(f) Explain the purpose of timesheet management in the context of project management software.

3

(g) Define the term Search Engine in the context of Internet. Explain spidering and indexing actions performed by a search engine. 5

(h) Explain the uses of radio waves and micro-waves for data transmission. 4

(i) Explain the purpose of any four folders used in an email account. 7

2. (a) Explain the need of memory hierarchy with the help of an example. Explain the advantages and disadvantages of using CD-ROM as a secondary storage device. 6

(b) What is the role of Operating System of a computer ? Define the term "Kernel" of an operating system. What are the uses of GUI and Input/Output control system for an operating system user ? 8

(c) How can Moodle be used for e-learning ? List the advantages and disadvantages of e-learning. 6

3. Compare and contrast any five of the following : 5x4=20

(a) Ring topology and Star topology

(b) Social networking and Blogging

(c) Macro and Functions in the context of spreadsheets.

(d) Compiler and Assembler

(e) Laser printing and Inkjet printing

(f) Mouse and Graphics tablet

4. (a) How do you define the access time on a magnetic disk ? Explain with the help of an example. Why is access time of magnetic tape higher than magnetic disk ? Explain. 6

(b) Explain the purpose of TCP/IP protocols. Also explain the concept of IP addresses and web addresses, with the help of an example of each. 7

(c) Explain the concepts of one-diniensional array with the help of an example. 4

(d) Explain the conditional statement with the help of an example. 3

5. Explain any five of the following with the help of an example/diagram, if required : 5x4=20

(a) Uses of any two utility softwares

(b) Configuration of a laptop computer

(c) Supercomputer

(d) Open source software

(e) Time-sharing system

(f) Computer virus

(g) Firewall in the context of networking

(h) Characteristics of Metropolitan Area Network (MAN)

BACHELOR OF COMPUTER APPLICATIONS

(BCA) (Revised)

Chapter 9: Term-End Examination, December, 2018

BCS-011 : COMPUTER BASICS AND PC SOFTWARE

Time : 3 hours

Maximum Marks :100

(Weightage : 75%)

Note: (i) Question No. 1 is compulsory.

(ii) Attempt any three Questions from the rest.

1. (a) A hypothetical simple computer has the following opcodes in its instruction set, each of which takes two operands that are given in the next 2 bytes :

(i) 00 Add (op1 + op2)

(ii) 01 Subtract (opt — op2)

(iii) 10 Multiply (op 1 x op2)

(iv) 11 Divide (opl op2)

(v) Write, in binary, the instruction that will carry out the calculation 46 x 75. 6

(b) Explain Internet Protocol addressing with the help of an example. 3

(c) Draw a flowchart that takes "n" numbers as input and produces the smallest of those numbers as output. 5

(d) Draw the graph for the following :

(i) Analog signal

(ii) Digital signal

(e) List any three features of cloud computing and describe each of them briefly. 5

(f) (i) What are the advantages and disadvantages of using CD as secondary storage ? 6

(ii) A tape is 4000 feet long and has a recording density of 1200 bpi. What is its storage capacity ?

(g) List five security measures one should take while browsing. 4

(h) What is an open source software ? Give examples. What are the advantages and disadvantages of using open source software ? 4

2. (a) What is perverse software and what are its effects ? Describe briefly any three types of perverse software. 6

(b) What is an unguided media channel ? Explain the characteristics of the different kinds of unguided media channels. 9

(c) What is a sequential access memory device ? Describe its features. 5

3. (a) Discuss the following in brief : 8

(i) Repeater

(ii) Bridge

(iii) Hub

(iv) Switch

(b) IGNOU needs to send a letter to each student of the BCS-011 course, informing them of the location of their examination centre. The major portion of the text is the same for each student, but the roll number, name of the student and examination centre location are different. These details are available in a data file for each student (one file with all the data). What are the steps you would follow to make a personalized letter in Microsoft Word for each student so that each one feels the letter has been drafted for him or her alone ? 8

(c) Explain the four different types of computer monitors. 4

4. (a) What is e-mail ? Describe its advantages and the facilities it provides. Explain how one can create an e-mail account on the e-mail system of one's choice. 8

(b) Describe the mainframe software architecture. Contrast it with the following, bringing out any underlying similarities : 8

(i) Two-tiered architecture

(ii) Three-tiered architecture n-tiered architecture

(c) What is Unicode ? Where and how is it used ? 4

5. Explain any five of the following with the help of examples or diagrams wherever required : 5x4=20

(a) Laptop computer

(b) Internet based software architecture

(c) Social networking

(d) Dot matrix printer

(e) Looping statements in programming languages

(f) Von Neumann architecture

(g) Routers

BACHELOR OF COMPUTER APPLICATIONS

(BCA) (Revised)

Chapter 10: Term-End Examination, June, 2019

BCS-011 : COMPUTER BASICS AND PC SOFTWARE

Time : 3 hours

Maximum Marks :100

(Weightage : 75%)

Note: (i) Question No. 1 is compulsory.

(ii) Attempt any three Questions from the rest.

1. (a) Your computer has an IP address of 202.41.15.57. You are planning to communicate with a computer on the same network that has an IP address of 202.4.1.15.116. What is the subnet mask ? 4

(b) What is the OSI model ? List the layers of the model from the lowest layer upwards. 4

(c) Write down the 9 logical and relational operators in C, giving the function of each. 5

(d) What is a compiler ? Draw a diagram showing the different stages of the program compilation process.

(e) Let x = 6 and y = 5. What are the values of 5

(i) x! = y

(ii) x < y

(iii) x % y

(iv) (x > 6) I I (y ! = 5)

(f) What is meant by the configuration of a Personal Computer ? Write down the configuration of a typical workstation used for software development work. 6

(g) What is the desktop in a Personal Computer ? What are the items typically found in it ? 4

(h) List the five parts of a communication system and mention the role of each. 6

2. (a) Explain, with the help of a diagram, the process of developing content for an e-learning course. 8

(b) List the features of second and third generation computers. 6

(c) What is the function of the memory management system of a computer ? Explain the primary tasks it needs to perform. 6

3. (a) Discuss the following briefly : 8

(i) Batch processing

(ii) Online processing Diskless workstations

(iv) Operating system kernel

(b) Describe the structured and modular design paradigm with the help of a diagram and pseudo code. 8

(c) What is volunteer computing ? Give an example of such computing. 4

4. (a) Draw the block diagram of a computer system and briefly explain the function of each of the main components. 8

(b) What is a linker ? Explain its function with the help of a diagram. 4

(c) Describe each of the following communication modes, bringing out the similarities and differences among them :

(i) Broadcast 8

(ii) Simplex

(iii) Half-duplex

(iv) Duplex

5. Explain any five of the following with the help of examples or diagrams wherever required : 5x4=20

(a) Hark disk defragmenter utility

(b) Video card of a Personal Computer

(c) Timesheet Management System

(d) Ring network topology

(e) Device drivers

(f) Infra-red communication

(g) Magnetic ink character recognition

BACHELOR OF COMPUTER APPLICATIONS

(BCA) (Revised)

Chapter 11: Term-End Examination, December, 2019

BCS-011 : COMPUTER BASICS AND PC SOFTWARE

Time : 3 hours

Maximum Marks :100

(Weightage : 75%)

Note: (i) Question No. 1 is compulsory.

(ii) Attempt any three Questions from the rest.

1 (a) Convert the following decimal numbers to equivalent binary number: 2

(i) 37

(ii) 0.125

(b) Convert the following hexadecimal number to equivalent binary : 2

(c) What will the storage capacity of a disk of 2.5 inch diameter 8 plates (16 recording surfaces) with 512 sectors per track and 2048 tracks per recording surface ? Assume that one sector can store 1048 bytes of data. 2

(d) Differentiate between the parallel port and serial port of a computer. 4

(e) What is an integrated circuit ? Is microprocessor an integrated circuit ? 2

(f) Explain the concept of memory hierarchy with the help of a diagram. 4

(g) Draw a flowchart to find if the given number is odd. 5

(h) What is the file management in the context to operating system ? How does file management system keeps track of a file ? Explain. 5

(i) What is the role of compiler in a computer system ? 3

(j) Which of the following are valid IPv4 address ? Give justification : 3

(i) 256.0.0.0

(ii) 192.168.1.27

(iii) 10.0.5.7.5

(k) What is meant by the term 'Network Topology' ? Explain the bus topology with the help of a diagram. List the advantages and disadvantages of bus topology. 6

(1) What is e-Learning ? What are its advantages and disadvantages ? 4

2. (a) Explain the three modes of data transmission. 5

(b) What is URL ? Why is it needed ? Explain various parts of a URL with the help of an example. How URL is translated to physical address of the resource ? Explain with the help of an example. 8

(c) Explain the following terms in the context of a search engine : 2+3+2 = 7

(i) Spidering or Web Crawling

(ii) Indexing

(iii) Searching

3. (a) What is Computer Virus ? How is it different from Trojan Horse in the context of a computer ? List the ways to counter the perverse software. 7

(b) Explain the following features of an application software : 8

(i) Mail merge in word processing

(ii) Macros in spreadsheet

(iii) Defining relationship in Database Management System

(iv) Scheduling in Project Management Software

(c) Differentiate between the open source software and proprietary software. 5

4. (a) Explain the role of various components of a computer system with the help of a diagram. 5

(b) Differentiate between the following 10

(i) Serial Access and Random Access

(ii) RAM and ROM

(iii) SRAM and DRAM

(iv) ROM and PROM

(v) Inkjet Printer and Laser Printer

(c) What are utility software ? Explain the use of disk checker and disk defragmenter utility software.

5. Explain any five of the following with the help of an example/diagram, if needed : 5x 4=20

(a). Web Browser

(b) Optical Memories

(c) ASCII and Unicode

(d) Looping Statement

(e) Kernel of an Operating System

(f) Linker and Text Editors

(g) Hub and Switches (Networking devices)

(h) WIKI

BACHELOR OF COMPUTER APPLICATIONS

(BCA) (Revised)

Chapter 12: Term-End Examination, June, 2020

BCS-011 : COMPUTER BASICS AND PC SOFTWARE

Time : 3 hours

Maximum Marks :100

(Weightage : 75%)

Note: (i) Question No. 1 is compulsory.

(ii) Attempt any three Questions from the rest.

1 (a) Convert the following numbers as asked: 6

(i) (0.375)10 to equivalent binary

(ii) (1010 1101)2 to equivalent decimal

(iii) (F2B)16 to equivalent binary

(iv) (1001 1401)2 to equivalent hexadecimal

(b). A computer system has CPU that processes data and input/output devices that perform the job of Input and Output of data, then why does a computer need RAM which is just a temporary memory ? 4

(c) Explain the characteristics of I/O devices that will be needed for the following : 4

(i) A printed page is to be converted to electronic form without retyping it.

(ii) A printed bill has bar-code, which is to be read to get all the payment details.

(iii) A device that xvill print very high quality and high precision graphs and pictures of different sizes.

(iv) A device that is required to record voice.

(d) What is the role of operating system ? Explain the role of memory management in operating system. 4

(e) You need to write a program in a programming language like C or C++ and execute it using your computer. Which software will you need for this purpose ? List the features of all the software that you will need to do so. 5

(f) Draw a flow chart to input three numbers and find the largest amongst them. 5

(g) What are the characteristics of optical fiber cable ? What are the advantages and disadvantages of optical fiber ? 4

(h) What is the role of DNS ? Explain with the help of an example. 4

(i) Explain the role of any two folders that are part of your e-mail account. 4

2. (a) Explain data organization of a disk with the help of diagram(s). 6

(b) What is an open source software ? Explain open source development model. 6

(c) Explain the role of the following network devices : 8

(i) Network Interface Card

(ii) Modem

(iii) Hub

(iv) Router

3. Compare and contrast • any five of the following : 6 x 4 = 20

(a) SRAM and DRAM

(b) Parallel port and. Serial port

(c) Subroutines and Functions

(d) Word processing and Spreadsheet software

(e) Primary search engines and Meta search engines

(f) Microwave transmission and Infrared transmission

4. (a) What is collaboration in the context of Web application ? What is Wild ? What are its characteristics ? List various activities for which Wiki can be used. 6

(b) What is cloud computing ? Discuss key features of cloud computing. 6

(c) Explain the Von Neumann architecture of a computer with the help of a diagram. 5

(d) What is an Integrated circuit ? What are the advantages of using Integrated circuits ? 3

5. (a) What is op-code in an Instruction of a computer ? Explain with the help of an example. 3

(b) Give one example each of volatile and non- volatile memory. 2

(c) What is the role of video card of a computer ? 2

(d) What are the uses of mail merge feature of word processor ? Explain with the help of an example. 5

(e) Explain the term batch processing in the context of operating system. 3

(f) What is a browser ? What are its features ? How does a browser communicate with web server ? 5

BACHELOR OF COMPUTER APPLICATIONS

(BCA) (Revised)

Chapter 13: Term-End Examination, December, 2020

BCS-011 : COMPUTER BASICS AND PC SOFTWARE

Time : 3 hours **Maximum Marks :100**

(Weightage : 75%)

Note: (i) Question No. 1 is compulsory.

(ii) Attempt any three Questions from the rest.

1. (a) Perform the following: 6

(i) Convert the following(16.25)10to binary.

(ii) Convert the number(1011 1010)2 to decimal.

(iii) Convert the number 16 (ABC) to binary.

(iv) Convert the number 2 (110011 1001) to hexadecimal.

(b) List the input/output devices for the following situations. Also describe the features of the device : 4

(i) For taking photographs

(ii) Producing output of photograph

(iii) Input of voice

(iv) Output of voice

(c) What is the role of main memory in a Computer ? Why is it called RAM ? How is RAM different from ROM ? 4

(d) You have attached a new printer to your computer. Which software will you require so that printer is installed correctly and starts to print. List features of the required computer software. 3

(e) Draw a flowchart for a program to find the average marks of the students of a class in a subject. The class strength is 15. 5

(f) List six operations that can be performed using a word processor. 3

(g) Explain the characteristics of hub and a router. Which of the two will be needed if your want to connect from one network to another ? 5

(h) What is an IPv4 address ? What are its components ? What is the use of a subnet mask ? Explain with help of an example. 6

(i) What is a Browser ? Why is it needed ? List any two features of a browser. 4

2. (a) What is the role of Arithmetic Logic Unit (ALU) and Control Unit (CU) in a computer ? 4

(b) What is a Super Computer ? How is it different to mainframe computer ? 4

(c) What are the uses of magnetic tape ? Explain, how is the access mechanism of magnetic tape different than that of magnetic disks. 4

(d) Explain the terms pixel, resolution and LEDs in the context of computer monitors. 4

(e) Explain the role of "Recycle Bin" and "Taskbar" on windows operating system. 4

3. (a) What are various components of a Local Area Network (LAN) ? What are the advantages of using LANs ? How are LAN different than WANs ? 6

(b) Explain the ring topology with the help of a diagram. List the advantages and disadvantages of ring topology. 6

(c) Explain the following web application giving their features and advantages : 8

(i) E-learning

(ii) E-mail

4. (a) What is a Computer Virus ? What role can anti-virus software play to control a computer virus ? 4

(b) What are open source software ? What are the primary objectives of open source movement ? 4

(c) What Graphical User Interface ? What are advantages of using these interfaces ? 4

(d) Explain the terms subroutine and function in the context of programming languages with the help of an example each. 5

(e) What is meant by Macros in the context of spreadsheet software ? Why are they needed ? 3

5. Discuss the uses of any eight of the following in a computer system/networking : 2 *1/2 × 8 = 20

(i) Firewall

(ii) TCP/IP Protocol

(iii) Radio waves

(iv) Twisted Pair Cable

(v) Compiler

(vi) Linker

(vii) Presentation Software

(viii) Database Management

(ix) ASCII

(x) DVD

(xi) Mouse

(xii) Bar code reader

BACHELOR OF COMPUTER APPLICATIONS

(BCA) (Revised)

Chapter 14: Term-End Examination, June, 2021

BCS-011 : COMPUTER BASICS AND PC SOFTWARE

Time : 3 hours

Maximum Marks :100

(Weightage : 75%)

Note: (i) Question No. 1 is compulsory.

(ii) Attempt any three Questions from the rest.

1. (a) Convert the following numbers as asked:

6

(i) (12.5)10 to binary

(ii) (1110 1000)2 to decimal

(iii) (01111111000)2 to hexadecimal

(iv) (BE5)16 TO binary

(b) Why does a computer need main memory? What is cache memory? How is main memory different from a cache memory?

5

(c) What are the advantages and disadvantages of using Inkjet printers?

6

(d) Draw a flow chart to find the sum of the first n natural numbers.

5

(e) A University wants to maintain, manipulate and organise large student data. Which software will be needed by the University ? Give justification in detail.

5

(f) Explain the Internet-based architecture of software with the help of a diagram.

4

(g) What are the different domains used in Web addresses ? How is an IP addressdifferent from a Web address ?

4

(h) What is a Browser ? What is a Cookie ? Is cookie a threat to information security or privacy ? Justify your answer.

4

(i) List and explain any two processes that are part of e-learning systems.

4

2. (a) Identify the Net ID and Device ID for the following IP address and Subnet mask pairs :

4

(i) 192.168.5.97 and 255·255.255.0

(ii)10.10.13.10 and 255.255.0.0

(b) How does the search on keyword ''Intelligent'' OR ''System'' differ from the search ''Intelligent'' AND ''System'' ? Explain.

3

(c) What is a MODEM ? Why is it used in networking ? Explain.

4

(d) Explain the characteristics and advantages of Wide Area Network (WAN).

4

(e) What are the characteristics of Twisted Pair Cable ? Compare its features with optical fibre cables.

5

3. (a) Explain how object-oriented software design paradigm is different from structured and modular design paradigm.

4

(b) What is the need of an Operating System ? Give names of two popular operating systems. Suppose you want to transfer a file from your hard disk to a CD, which of the following services of the operating system will be used and for what purpose ? (User Interface, File management, Input/Output services, Process control management and

Memory management)

8

(c) Explain which software will be required to perform the following tasks. Also list four features of these software.

8

(i) Scheduling of tasks

(ii) Creating mailmerge

(iii) Entering formulas and functions

(iv) Creating presentation

4. (a) Explain the working of a basic computer with the help of a diagram showing its basic components.

6

(b) What are the differences between primary and secondary memory of a computer. Which of them is larger in size ? Which of them is faster ?

6

(c) Explain the role of the following utility software :

4

(i) Disk checkers

(ii) System restore

(d) What is the use of digitizing (graphic) tablet and joystick ?

4

5. Explain any five of the following with the help of an example/a diagram : 5 x 4=20

(a) Supercomputer

(b) Fourth Generation Computers

(c) Disk Layout of a CD-ROM

(d) Perverse Software

(e) Open-source Software

(f) Wiki

(g) TCP/IP

BACHELOR OF COMPUTER APPLICATIONS
(BCA) (Revised)

Chapter 15: Term-End Examination, June, 2022

BCS-011 : COMPUTER BASICS AND PC SOFTWARE

Time : 3 hours

Maximum Marks :100

(Weightage : 75%)

Note: (i) Question No. 1 is compulsory.

(ii) Attempt any three Questions from the rest.

1. (a) Perform the following operations:

5

(i) Convert (235)10 to binary

(ii) Convert (10/3750)10 to binary

(iii) Convert (1011101)2 to decimal

(iv) Convert (FABC) 16 to binary

(v) Convert (A5)16 to decimal

(b) What will be the storage capacity of a 2.5 inch diameter disc pack having 4 plates with each surface of the plate having 2048 tracks and each tracks having 512 sectors? A sector can store 1024 bytes of data.

(c) Explain the von Neumann Architecture with the help of a diagram.

4

(d) Explain two features of the software that will be needed for each of the following operations :

6

(i) Keeping track of files and directories.

(ii) Translating high level language program to machine language.

(iii) Identify and remove computer virus.

(e) Write an algorithm and draw the flowchart for finding the sum of the first 10 odd numbers.

7

(f) Given the following IP addresses and Subnet mask, find the Net-ID :

3

(i) IP address 10.1.5.7 with subnet mask 255.0.0.0

(ii) IP address 192.168.1.05 with subnet mask 255.255.255.0

(g) Explain the purpose of the following Networking devices. :

6

(i) Network Interface Card

(ii) Modem

(iii) Repeater

(h) List any six advantages of e-learning.

3

(i) List two advantages and one disadvantage of using Inkjet Printer.

3

2. (a) Define the term Instruction in the context of a computer processor. Explain the role of control unit for execution of an instruction.

5

(b) Differentiate between the following :

10

(i) Static RAM and Dynamic RAM

(ii) RAM and ROM

(iii) Hard disk and Magnetic tapes

(iv) DVD and CD

(c) What is the role of a port in a computer ? Explain the use of (i) Parallel port, and (ii) Serial port in a computer.

5

3. (a) Explain the terms client and server in the context of client/server architecture. Explain the three-tier client/server architecture with the help of a diagram.

5

(b) What is an Open-source Software ? List any two objectives of an Open-source movement. List the name and purpose of any four Open-source Software.

5

(c) Define the following in the context of an Operating System :

6

(i) Batch Processing

(ii) Graphical User Interface

(iii) Multiprogramming

(iv) Time-Sharing System

(d) Given the values of three variables as x = 5, y = 8 and z = 13, what would be the output of the following expressions in C programming language ?

4

(i) x = = y

(ii) (x + y) = = z

(iii) y < z

(iv) x ! = z

4. (a) Explain the terms in the context of Computer Network :

6

(i) Half Duplex

(ii) Channel

(iii) Packet Switching

(iv) Bandwidth

(b) Explain the characteristics of Local Area Networks. How are LANs different from WANs ?

5

(c) What is a URL in the context of Internet ? Explain with the help of an example. Also explain the role of DNS with the help of an example.

4

(d) Explain the characteristics of the following :

5

(i) WIKI

(ii) Social Networking

5. Explain any five of the following with the help of an example or a diagram, wherever required : 5 x 4=20

(a) Security Threats on Internet

(b) TCP/IP Model

(c) Object-Oriented Programming Language

(d) Perverse Software

(e) Subroutine and Functions

(f) Memory Hierarchy

(g) Classification of Printers

(h) Features of Spreadsheet Software

BACHELOR OF COMPUTER APPLICATIONS

(BCA) (Revised)

Chapter 16: Term-End Examination, December, 2022

BCS-011 : COMPUTER BASICS AND PC SOFTWARE

Time : 3 hours

Maximum Marks :100

(Weightage : 75%)

Note: (i) Question No. 1 is compulsory.

(ii) Attempt any three Questions from the rest.

1. (a) Do the following conversions:

8

(i) $(37.5)_{10}$ to binary

(ii) $(100100101101)_2$ to Hexadecimal

(iii) $(ABE)_{16}$ to Binary

(iv) $(574)_8$ to Decimal

(b) What is main memory of the computer and why is it needed ? Explain briefly the various types of main memory.

5

(c) Why are the arrays used in programming ? Explain with the help of an example of one-dimensional array.

3

(d) Differentiate between the following :

6

(i) Subroutine and Function

(ii) Modem and Router

(iii) URL and IP address

(e) What are communication ports and why are they needed ? Explain parallel ports and serial ports.

5

(f) Why do computer systems need Antivirus Softwares ? Which technique do antivirus programs use to identify viruses ?

5

(g) Write short notes on the following :

8

(i) E-learning

(ii) Security threats on Internet

2. (a) What is CPU ? Describe the structure of the CPU and explain its components with the help of a diagram.

8

(b) What is Operating System ? What kind of services does operating system provide to users and programs ?

6

(c) How does data get transmitted via unguided transmission media ? Explain the radio, microwave and infrared modes of wireless transmission.

6

3. (a) What are Optical Memories ? Explain briefly any four types of optical disks.

8

(b) What is cloud computing ? Explain the various cloud services and how they benefit organizations. Describe key features and benefits of cloud based solutions.

7

(c) What are open source software and why are they in demand ? List the key criterion of OSD compliance.

5

4. (a) Discuss the key characteristics of printers on the basis of quality of print.

4

(b) What are utility softwares ? Explain the following utility softwares :

10

(i) Disk Defragmenter

(ii) CHKDSK

(iii) Data compression

(iv) Disk management

(c) Describe the TCP/IP model with the help of a diagram.

6

5. (a) Draw a flowchart to find whether a given number is even or odd.

6

(b) What is software project management ? Explain various project management activities.

8

(c) What is mail merge ? Explain various steps of mail merge with the help of an example.

6

BACHELOR OF COMPUTER APPLICATIONS

(BCA) (Revised)

Chapter 17: Term-End Examination, June, 2023

BCS-011 : COMPUTER BASICS AND PC SOFTWARE

Time : 3 hours

Maximum Marks :100

(Weightage : 75%)

Note: (i) Question No. 1 is compulsory.

(ii) Attempt any three Questions from the rest.

1. (a) Write short notes on the following:

10

(i) Cache memory

(ii) PROM

(iii) Winchester disc

(iv) WORM

(v) WIKI

(b) Describe the need and working of any two input devices.

4

(c) What are Operating Systems ? Explain any four operating system services.

6

(d) Explain the differences between wired and wireless communication.

5

(e) What is the need of MS-Excel Software ? List any four features of this software.

5

(f) What are Network Topologies ? Explain Star and Bus topologies with the help of a diagram.

6

(g) What are IP Addresses ? Describe the components of an IPv4 Address.

4

2. (a) List the key features of the technologies used in the five generations of computer evolution.

5

(b) What is Data Communication ? Draw and explain various components of a simple data communication system.

7

(c) What are cookies ? Are they dangerous for your system ? List some tips to avoid cookies.

5

(d) Write a short note on Proxy Servers.

3

3. (a) What is seek time ? How is it different from latency time ?

5

(b) Describe the storage organization of a Hard Disk Drive with the help of a diagram.

8

(c) What is Open Source Software ? Explain the main features of the Open Source Development Model.

7

4. (a) Differentiate between CRT, LCD and LED monitors.

6

(b) What is Client/Server Architecture ? Explain the three-tier client/server architectures with the help of a diagram.

7

(c) Describe the OSI reference model with the help of a diagram.

7

5. (a) Why does software need licence ? Explain the evolution of software licencing and the different types of software licences.

9

(b) What are perverse software ? Explain any four perverse softwares and how can users counter and control such softwares in their systems.

6

(c) What are collaboration tools and why are they needed ? Describe any two web based collaboration tools.

5

BACHELOR OF COMPUTER APPLICATIONS

(BCA) (Revised)

Chapter 18: Term-End Examination, December, 2023

BCS-011 : COMPUTER BASICS AND PC SOFTWARE

Time : 3 hours

Maximum Marks :100

(Weightage : 75%)

Note: (i) Question No. 1 is compulsory.

(ii) Attempt any three Questions from the rest.

1. (a) Convert the following as asked :

6

(i) (0.0125)10 to equivalent binary

(ii) (10011111)2 to equivalent decimal

(iii) (FA5)16 to equivalent binary

(iv) (1001 0110 1110)2 to equivalentvhexadecimal

(b) A computer system has large RAM, still itvrequires secondary storage. Why ? Explain.

4

(c) Explain the use and characteristics of the following input-output devices :

4

(i) Bar Code Reader

(ii) Speaker and Microphone

(d) Explain why an operating system is needed in a computer system. Differentiate between the system software and application software.

5

(e) What is an algorithm ? What are the three control statements in the context of algorithm ? Explain each statement with the help of an example.

7

(f) List any two features of a spreadsheet software.

2

(g) Explain the ring topology of local area networks. List its advantages and disadvantages.

6

(h) Explain the purpose of any four folders that are available in an email software.

4

(i) List any four features of a social networking website.

2

2. (a) What are the different components of a computer ? Explain the role of each component with the help of a diagram.

6

(b) Differentiate between the following :

8

(i) CD-ROM and Hard disk

(ii) Seek time and Latency time in the context of access time

(iii) Cache memory and Main memory

(iv) Transistor and Vacuum tube

(c) What is a port ? Explain the uses of parallel port, serial port, universal serial bus and SCSI port.

6

3. (a) Explain the three-tier client-server architecture with the help of a diagram.

5

(b) What is multiprogramming ? How is it different from batch processing ? Explain.

5

(c) Explain the concept of one-dimensional and two-dimensional arrays with the help of an example pseudo code of each.

5

(d) Explain the features of word processing application.

5

4. (a) Explain the characteristics of a Wide Area Network. How is a WAN different to a LAN ? Explain.

5

(b) What is the need of TCP/IP ? What is a URL ? How is URL different to an IP address ? Explain with the help of an example.

5

(c) What is the role of a browser software ? What is a search engine ? How does a search engine collects information about web page ?

5

(d) What are the characteristics of a WIKI ? What are the different advantages of using a WIKI ?

5

5. Explain the following with the help of a diagram/example; if needed :

5×4=20

(a) Features of E-learning

(b) Perverse Software

(c) Features of project management software

(d) Different types of printers

(e) Disk checkers and disk defragmenters

9 789369 725007

Printed at Repro India Ltd.